Charles Cuthbert Hall

Does God send trouble?

An earnest effort to discern between Christian tradition and Christian truth

Charles Cuthbert Hall

Does God send trouble?
An earnest effort to discern between Christian tradition and Christian truth

ISBN/EAN: 9783742836748

Manufactured in Europe, USA, Canada, Australia, Japan

Cover: Foto ©Lupo / pixelio.de

Manufactured and distributed by brebook publishing software (www.brebook.com)

Charles Cuthbert Hall

Does God send trouble?

Does God send Trouble?

*AN EARNEST EFFORT TO DISCERN BE-
TWEEN CHRISTIAN TRADITION AND
CHRISTIAN TRUTH*

BY

CHARLES CUTHBERT HALL, D. D.
MINISTER OF THE FIRST PRESBYTERIAN CHURCH OF BROOKLYN, N. Y.

'Ο Θεὸς ἀγάπη ἐστίν
1 Epistle of St. John, iv. 16

BOSTON AND NEW YORK
HOUGHTON, MIFFLIN AND COMPANY
The Riverside Press, Cambridge

TO ALL
WHO SORROW OVER
THE SORROWS OF HUMANITY.

INTRODUCTORY NOTE.

THE thoughts which make this little book are not the outcome of a sudden impulse. They are now presented with a desire to glorify Him Who came to bear our griefs and to carry our sorrows, and in the hope of cheering those who suffer in this present evil world.

If this book shall appear to some who read it only a departure from the current teaching, perhaps also to others it shall seem to suggest an approach to the better understanding of God's Love.

BROOKLYN, 27 *January*, 1894.

CONTENTS.

CHAPTER I.
THE PROBLEM OF CONSOLATION 1

CHAPTER II.
THE RELATION OF GOD TO NATURAL LAW, TO CHASTISEMENT, AND TO DISCIPLINE 21

CHAPTER III.
THE HISTORIC ATONEMENT AND THE PUNISHMENT OF SIN 39

CHAPTER IV.
THE WILL OF GOD AND THE TENDENCY OF NATURE 55

CHAPTER V.
THE DUTY, THE COMFORT, AND THE POWER OF PRAYER 75

CHAPTER I.

THE PROBLEM OF CONSOLATION.

Are the consolations of God too small for thee? BOOK OF JOB
(Revised Version).

DOES GOD SEND TROUBLE?

CHAPTER I.

THE PROBLEM OF CONSOLATION.

In the old Book of Job, Eliphaz the Temanite is represented as asking the suffering patriarch, who rejects such sympathy as is offered: "Are the consolations of God too small for thee?" That question continues to have a place and a meaning as long as Humanity continues to bear its solemn burden of suffering. All who suffer, whether in mind, in body, or in estate, instinctively know whether the consolations of God are or are not too small for them; whether the thought of God brings to them any peace and strength in their troubles, or whether the thought of God is to them an empty, uninspiring thought, and the consolations of God are too small and too inadequate to slake the thirstings of the afflicted heart. "Are the consolations of God too small for thee?" Oh, wonderful question, thrilling, not with reproof, but with sympathy and with the desire to help! The cold, hard ring of the voice of Job's miserable comforter has died out of this question long ago; and to-day it is spoken in a voice richly tender as that of Christ Himself, spoken gently, yea, reverently to all to whom sorrow seems so great, that God seems too small; life's sadness broad, the consolations of God narrow.

In the Old Testament Scriptures, one in Genesis, one in Jeremiah, are two word-pictures whose pathos might make an angel weep: the one is the grief of Jacob; the other is the grief of Rachel. "Jacob mourned for his son. And all his sons and all his daughters rose up to comfort him; but he refused to be comforted; and he said: For I will go down into the grave unto my son, mourning." "A voice is heard in Ramah, lamentation and bitter weeping, Rachel weeping for her children; she refuseth to be comforted for her children, because they are not." "He refused to be comforted." "She refuseth to be comforted." The consolations offered were too small, they could not meet the vaster need, nor measure across the chasm of a broken heart. Whoever goes out among lives to-day, not as a spectator, a critic, or a cynic, but as a confidant and a friend, will find many who refuse to be comforted; not because they want to be unhappy, but because nothing they meet or hear is great enough to appeal to them, or mighty enough to lift them. Consolations, alike of man and of God, are too small to perform their intended office.

It is perfectly useless and illogical to say to those who refuse to be comforted that they *ought* to be comforted. For comfort, relief in sorrow (on the part of the afflicted), is not an act which one puts forth one's hand and does; comfort is a state of mind into which one is brought by the operation of adequate causes. If you bring to a person a form of consolation and it fails to comfort, it is folly to say: You *ought* to be comforted by this. The fact is that for some reason or other the consolation you have brought is too small; it is inadequate, or it is inapplicable. To blame persons for continuing to be sad, for refusing to be comforted after you have brought to their attention what you believe to be an adequate consolation, is absurd. A physician calls upon his patient at night, carefully looks him over, and prescribes powders. "Let these be given," he says, "at intervals of two hours throughout the night, and I believe that in the morning I shall find him better." In the morning the physician returns, finds that his patient has faithfully taken the powders, and is much worse. What will the doctor do? Will he turn on his patient and say: "You ought to be better. It is wrong for you to refuse to get better. I gave you the right powders, and here you are worse this morning." If a doctor spoke thus to his patient, he would be a fool. What possible obligation exists for the man to be better if the powders did not make him better? Nay; the physician would say: "This man is worse. I gave him what I believed was adequate. Either I gave him the wrong medicine, or conditions have developed in himself to counteract the influence of the right medicine. I must study the case until I find what will reach him, arrest the waste of tissue, and stimulate the weakened forces of repair and recovery." If consolations do not comfort, blame not the heart that weeps on, commit not the folly of saying that a heart *ought* to be comforted by thoughts which do not appeal to it; that tears can be dried on demand; that burdens can be lifted from the heart, unless there are given strong consolations, like strong hands, to grapple with those burdens and to lift them.

When even the consolations of God seem too small for one who suffers, seek for the causes of that strange insufficiency. There was a reason why the medicine helped not the sick man. And there are always reasons why God's consolations fail to console.

Consolation is a problem. Many would-be consolers work at it in vain; though working in God's name, His consolations seem in their hands ineffective and barren. And many who sorely need the richest consolations of God never obtain them.

For years I have pondered these facts intently and continuously. Living so much as it has been my privilege to live among the sorrowing and the distressed, I have been amazed to find how few, of all who suffer, know the richness of the consolations of God. There is much submission to God's will, as it is called; though often the term "God's will" is applied to troubles which are the Devil's will rather than "God's will." There is much reverent wonder at the reasons why afflictions are sent by God upon men, when of many of those afflictions it is certain God did not send them, but that they were instead the direct result of human carelessness, or of human extravagance, or of human hatefulness, or of human lustfulness. And there is far down in many a heart that has suffered a deep-set, though surreptitious protest against "the will of God," as it is called, which sent this sickness, or that loss of property, or this disappointment, or that bereavement; when not one of those sorrows, the sickness, the loss of property, the disappointment, the bereavement, came from God's will, but from that broken and bruised and halting and sin-stricken order of the fallen creation which broke away from God's dear will, and pierced itself through with many sorrows. And so, between all the suffering men and women who meekly submit to what they call "the will of God," and those who puzzle and wonder over what they call "the will of God," and those who secretly rebel against what they call "the will of God," it is not many, I fear, of all the great throng of suffering hearts, who know in their broad fullness, in their immense tenderness, in their gladdening and ineffable sympathy, the meaning of the words: "*The consolations of God.*"

Human sympathy means much more to many people than Divine sympathy — and to not a few who have suffered, the beautiful self-sacrifice, the generosity, the pitiful love of blessed earthly friends, the labor and suffering those friends endure to save life, stand before their minds (though their tongues utter it not), as a kind of rebuking contrast to God, Who says He loves us, yet (as they say) robs us of our property, sends continual disappointment on us, and sweeps our helpless little children into their graves. Oh! if you could hear, as I have heard for years, the despairing groan from suffering hearts, asking those terrible, mistaken questions: "Why — why does God bring all this trouble on me? Why has He made my wife an invalid, or my child an imbecile? Why has He swept my fortune away? Why has He robbed me of the desire of my eyes? Why has He smitten me with this disease, so that my life is a burden to myself?" you would not wonder that I say: few, of all the many who suffer, comprehend the consolations of God; few know God's real attitude toward those who suffer; few live in such a spirit as permits them to realize the largeness, the sufficiency, the uplifting strength of the consolations of God. Through years of almost continual fellowship with sorrow, I have pondered this problem of consolation until it has seemed at times my heart would break with sympathy for those to whom God's consolations were too small. And in this little book I speak out my beliefs on this subject with a freedom born of no short-lived impulse, but of the prayer and the study of years.

I believe that for very many persons in and out of the Christian Church, the consolations of God are too small; that is, they do not console, they do not substantially alleviate sorrow, nor substantially assist in providing hopeful and cheering thoughts for the life that now is. In this respect the consolations of man are often more effective, and come nearer to the bruised spirit than do the consolations of God; and the most of men bear their sorrows by getting used to them, as the poor cart-horse bears at last, without flinching, the collar that galls his neck. Use, time, kind friends, and hard work do more for the many than God's consolations, to make the pains of life endurable. To account for such a state of things in part, there may doubtless be local causes, acting upon individuals, such as peculiarities of temperament, or of habit, or of family training, or of the friend environment. And all such local causes must be reckoned with by one who would solve the problem of consolation for any single life. But far above and beyond all local causes are *two general causes* which seem to have spread their influence far and wide in the common thought of the age, to have insinuated themselves into our ordinary phrases of speech, into our prayers, into our hymns, into our devotional literature, and to have brought about a popular conception of trouble, sorrow, sickness, and death (as things that come from God, things that God sends upon us), which has immensely weakened the power of God's consolations to console; which has made them unto many a troubled heart (to use the startling phrase of Eliphaz the Temanite) "too small." These two general causes are: first, a distorted view of God's relation to our sorrows; second, a consequently distorted relation of our life to God.

Out of a desire, doubtless, to proclaim the sovereignty of God over His creatures, and to recognize after some fashion His hand in all the events of life, a fearful perversion of God's true relation to human suffering, loss, sickness, and death has spread like an untimely frost over the minds of men, whereby all of these evils that so abound in our time are described as the dealings of God's will with the children of men. From Him, we are told, come these mysterious visitations, the pestilence that walketh in darkness; the destruction that wasteth at noonday; the railway crash that smites with sudden death the beloved head of an household and leaves a family in poverty; the financial calamity that melts a fortune in an hour; the insidious disease that fastens itself in the lungs of the strong, true-hearted man, and worries, wastes, and wears him away till he surrenders to the enemy he does not fear, going gallantly to his untimely grave; the fever that breaks out in the beautiful child, tortures its sweet life for one hideous week, then leaves the pure temple an unsightly and unapproachable ruin.

There is a kind of religious phraseology prevalent in our time which would seek to persuade us that it is God who has done these atrocities, that it is God who has wrecked this fortune; God who has made the strong man a consumptive, God who has seized that beauteous child, whose every motion was grace, whose every glance was ecstacy, and has tortured it deliberately to death. I have even heard a Christian friend suggest to a mother, sitting white as ashes by her dead baby, "Perhaps God saw you loved the child too much, and so He took it from you." If I believed that God spreads scarlet fever among little children; if I believed that God sweeps off into their graves so many young wives and mothers; if I believed that God produces idiots, or drives people mad, or makes men murder and steal and blast their families, I would hate Him as other men hate Him. Who that believes this can sincerely care for the consolations of God, or want them? If God is practically responsible for nine tenths of the evil and sorrow that come on us, what impulse have we to desire His consolations, save by an effort of religious duty? If you employed a physician who trifled with your child's life, and aggravated its disease till it died, would you go to that physician for comfort in your bereavement? But I believe none of this. I believe that God's whole and only intention for man was from eternity to give him a life as perfect, as free, as gloriously supreme over physical forces, as consummate in its joy as the life of God and of His Christ; that it was the eternal ideal of God for us, that we in our manhood should be conformed to the image of His Son. I believe that God, in introducing man to the earth, set him amidst conditions altogether fitted to produce perfect and everlasting happiness. There was no sickness, no disorder, no death. And the Heart of God rejoiced in His world: —

> "And a Priest's Hand through creation,
> Waved calm and consecration."

Then came sin. By man it came as its channel and its exponent. Sin is the perverted choice of a free being. And with sin came its train of consequences; all sorrow, all perversion of instincts and lusts, all confusion of interests, all strife and warfare, all sickness with its incredible train of infirmities, all debasement and derangement of the intellect, all degeneration of vitality, and that supreme, that heroic, that last catastrophe — *Death*. And God saw and sorrowed over the man He loved. God saw His beautiful creation blackened, and an anarchy springing up within His order: a Devil-motive and a Devil-mission penetrating everywhere, till the whole creation, once so happy and made for happiness, but self-destroyed through sin, groaned and travailed in pain. And God, hating Death as a contradiction of His purpose for man, so *loved* the world, He gave His only begotten Son that whosoever believeth in Him should not perish but have everlasting Life. God took man's part against the disorder that had broken out in the creation, to redeem and to rescue man from that disorder; to console and to strengthen his heart while waiting for deliverance. And God is on man's side to-day, as his best, his kindest Friend, taking his part *against* the woes and sorrows of life, taking his part against Death, and pledging Himself to us that Death shall not always have dominion over us. We *must* break away from our forms of popular speech which continually misrepresent and dishonor God in His relation to Death: we must teach ourselves to stop saying at the death-beds of our friends: "God is taking them away from us." God *hates* Death. Death is His enemy as much as ours. Death is a catastrophe and a blot on creation. God's proclamation against Death is explicit and oft repeated. Read it in the magnificent prophecy of Hosea: "I will ransom them from the power of the grave; I will redeem them from Death. O Death, I will be thy plagues. O Grave! I will be thy destruction." Death is not the outcome of God's will. Death is the outcome of natural law, the effect of natural causes, in a created order perverted and spoiled by sin. "By man sin entered into the world, and death by sin." Scarlet fever smites the temple of the dear child's body and leaves it a ruin. We torture our hearts to make them say this fearful paradox: "God's will has done this, therefore I turn to God to comfort me." How many hearts have bled, blasphemed, and broken in the excruciating effort to ask comfort from Him Who killed the child. We try to train ourselves to believe that this is "kissing the rod." We are wrong. "What took this child away?" Shall we say, the will of God? No, let us say the truth; bad drainage and germ-infection. And God sorrows with us as much as any earthly friends, for He no more did it than did they. What does it mean then: "The Lord gave and the Lord hath taken away, blessed be the name of the Lord"? The Hebrew word is clear: "The Lord gave and the Lord hath *received*, blessed be His name." Who could bless the Lord for taking away our beloved? But we can bless Him that since the sad and broken natural order of disease and death has conquered our loved one, the Lord has *received* to His eternal paradise the spirit we loved. Once only in the Bible, so far as I know, is it said of a human being: "God took him away," and that man was Enoch — who *did not die*. God for some reason made him an exception to the natural order. And to those who believe in the Pre-millennial Coming of our Lord, one of the bright thoughts about it is, that they who are living on the earth when He comes, as His disciples, shall be gathered to Him without death.

"They that remain, that are left, unto the Coming of the Lord shall be caught up to meet the Lord in the air; and so shall we ever be with the Lord." "We shall not all sleep."

God, then, being not the Author of our troubles, of our sicknesses, of our deaths, but looking upon all these things rather as sad and fearful interruptions of His plan for us, has sought to comfort man by pouring forth consolations into his life. And what are these consolations of God?

The Incarnation is one of God's consolations: that into the very midst of this broken order has entered in human form, with human sensibilities and human sympathies, the Lord Jesus Christ, to be tempted like as we are, to bear our griefs, to carry our sorrows, to taste death for every man, to show us in His Resurrection that there is victory in store for us; to lift up our eyes toward that new order, which is but the original order brought back across the chaos of sin and made once more the inheritance of redeemed Humanity: "I am the Resurrection and the Life: he that believeth in Me, though He were dead, yet shall he live; and whosoever liveth and believeth in Me shall never die."

The Divine Word is one of God's consolations. "Are the consolations of God too small for thee and the Word that dealeth gently with thee?" Such is the full reading of that splendid verse in Job. How gently deals the Word of God with all sorrowing hearts that hear and understand its truest meaning! How it urges us, counsels us, pleads with us, not to confuse these agonizing catastrophes of sin and death with the will and the heart of God! How it pleads with us not to mistake the Devil's malignant will for God's blessed will; not to load on God the responsibility for sorrows that are the offspring of sin! "*This* is the will of God," it says, " even your sanctification." And amidst the bitterness of our lot, in sorrow and death, it ever protests, " God has not done this — *God is Love.* Come to me, ye that are heavy laden, — *I* will give you rest."

The Holy Spirit is one of the consolations of God. The Comforter, the Strength-maker, the Paraclete, the Advocate is He; the ever present Friend; Revealer of the presence of the unseen Lord; Creator in our hearts of that vision of things to come, when the new order of redemption shall be consummated in the manifestation of the King, when this corruptible shall put on incorruption and this mortal shall put on immortality, when sorrow and sighing shall flee away, when Death shall be swallowed up in victory.

Two words as I close this chapter. What then is "chastisement," and what then is "discipline"? Both are words which undoubtedly have their immense reality in human experience. What is chastisement? Chastisement means "making chaste." What is the meaning of such a great passage as that in Hebrews, "Whom the Lord loveth He chasteneth, and scourgeth every son whom He receiveth"? I believe that that is spiritual and only spiritual. It is not a passage relating to bodily calamities. It is that intense experience of our spirits with the Father of our spirits, through which in our inward life we are rebuked and purified and made meet for the kingdom of God. Bodily calamities are only the results of natural laws. Every one of them can be traced to natural causes. The moment we call them chastisements, we plunge into confusion. Are the sufferings of infants chastisements? When the Spanish bomb-throwers kill by chance innocent women, are their orphaned children chastised by God? When the mistake of a British Admiral carries his stately flagship to the bottom of the Mediterranean, shall we tell the weeping wives, and children, and sisters, and mothers, and lovers in England that they are being chastised by the hand of God? God forbid! Bodily sin carries its own retribution to the sinner, under natural law; but chastisement from God, according to the Scripture, is a process of the spiritual life, not of the physical order. And what, then, is discipline? What does the word mean? It means "*Teaching.*" God can teach through anything, joy or sorrow, holiness or sin, life or death. Christ used anything and everything to serve His teaching purpose in His parables, — birds and flowers, or drunken servants and cheating clerks. And God takes everything, even all the events of this broken order of sin and sorrow, and through the use of it in the hand of His Holy Spirit He *teaches*. Thus out of sorrow, out of sickness, out of death, evils of the natural order, what magnificent lessons have been learned in the school of grace; what friendships have been formed beneath the Cross; what power for usefulness has sprung into being from the side of the grave! And the end of the whole matter is: *God is Love.* God is not the Author of confusion, but of peace. By man came death; by Christ have come life and power and hope; and to all who suffer in the flesh, God waits to be gracious, saying unto them continually, "As one whom his mother comforteth, so will I comfort you."

CHAPTER II.

THE RELATION OF GOD TO NATURAL LAW, TO CHASTISEMENT, AND TO DISCIPLINE.

Whatsoever a man soweth, that shall he also reap. — EPISTLE TO THE GALATIANS.

Whom the Lord loveth, He chasteneth. — EPISTLE TO THE HEBREWS.

It is enough for the disciple that he be as his Teacher. — GOSPEL OF ST. MATTHEW. (Revised Version and margin.)

CHAPTER II.

THE RELATION OF GOD TO NATURAL LAW, TO CHASTISEMENT, AND TO DISCIPLINE.

The proposition laid down in the preceding chapter suggests questions which lead the mind forth in many directions. If we permit ourselves to break away from the traditional language which teaches us to regard the troubles of our present life as sent from God, we find ourselves in the midst of thoughts full of vital interest. In an earnest effort to discern between Christian tradition and Christian truth, the teachings of the New Testament constitute the final court of appeal. The Christian Scriptures are authoritative for the definition of Christian truth. I believe in the perfect unity of that Divine Revelation which is contained in the two Testaments. Nevertheless, the Bible is used unfairly if used indiscriminately, *i. e.*, without regard to dispensational distinctions. In the study of every Biblical subject it is necessary to take into consideration the differences of view-point, of language, of time, of racial significance, of dispensational method between the Hebrew Scriptures and those Christian Scriptures which must be the immediate standard of revelation for ourselves.

The relation of God to Natural Law is one of the first subjects presented to the mind intent on discerning between tradition and truth in answering the question: "Does God send trouble?" This relation is pointed out in the inexorable verse from the Epistle to the Galatians: "Be not deceived, God is not mocked, for whatsoever a man soweth, that shall he also reap." I call this "the inexorable verse;" but "inexorable" does not mean "cruel," it means "unchangeable;" and there is as much blessing as pain in that thought. If natural laws were not inexorable, if they were changeful, erratic, and uncertain in their action, life would be intolerable, and this world one frightful chaos. No plans could then be made; no undertakings could be securely developed; the material and intellectual progress of the race comes to an end; society dissolves in physical anarchy for which it is not responsible; the sciences explode in ruins; the arts topple from their sinking foundations; the individual cowers before the cruel caprice of his Creator. The one beautiful remnant of the original creation which survives, towering like a sublime Greek peristyle above the heaping ruins of man's sinful life, is the inexorable, the unchangeable character of natural laws. The original order survives in the sequence of cause and effect, although the madness of sinning men has turned that fair order against themselves. "Natural Law," says Henry Drummond, "is an ascertained working sequence or constant order among the phenomena of Nature. Law is order. The Laws of Nature are simply statements of the orderly condition of things in Nature. They are modes of operation. They are great lines running out through the world, reducing it like parallels of latitude to intelligent order." There was a Hand that drew those lines. It was the same Hand that brought man to the earth and set him to live among those lines of order. The order was perfectly fit for man. Man was perfectly fit for the order. There was no place for catastrophe; no occasion for suffering; no cause nor intention of death. The God-made man was in the God-made order; and his entire life was adjusted to the circumjacent order as the eye to light, the ear to sound. The order stands unchanged. No new laws; no changed laws; no unjust laws. The same order. The man within the order *changed*. The order stands harmonious with itself; every law as beautiful, as beneficent to-day as at the beginning. The man has dropped out of harmony with the order. This is sin. Sin is lawlessness; wrong adjustment to right laws; wrong uses of right things. And this accounts for all the physical and material sorrow, sickness, misery, poverty, bitterness, violence, death in the world. "By man sin entered into the world and death by sin; and death passed upon all men, because all have sinned." Nothing is so easy as to make beautiful laws and beautiful things deadly by misuse and mismanagement, and to transmit the effects of our misuse, by processes of just and rightful law, to lives not only innocent, but ignorant of the misuse. Sin is misadjustment to law, and each new sin extorts one more abnormal consequence from a normal order; throws one more handful of dust into the troubled air, which in the fresh morning of the world was bright as crystal, revealing everywhere the Presence of God.

Keeping in the foreground of the mind this thought, that evil and death are not God's order, not of God's making, but are the effects of man's misadjustments of himself to inexorable laws of Nature, consider the two questions which are immediately asked: Cannot God readjust the natural order? And if He can, why does He not, and thus prevent suffering? To the first of these questions there can be but one answer for those who believe. That answer is "Yes." Do I believe in miracles? Surely I believe in miracles. Miracles are results of a character contrary to our experience, arising from the combining of natural laws in ways superior to the present order. From time to time, to secure certain ends, such as the authorization of a new revelation of truth, or the certifying of a new teacher of truth, miracles have occurred. They may occur again at the pleasure of God. Those who believe miracles believe that God can change the natural order if He will. The other question immediately presses: If He can change the order, why does He not, and thus prevent suffering? The answer which yields itself to reflection is a very solemn one. God does not change the natural order, because the natural order is the right order. Natural laws are the best laws for man as God made him. Natural laws are the lines of order drawn through a perfect world. The fault is not in them, but in the sinning race which has put itself in wrong relations to those laws.

The laws of Nature have not broken humanity. Humanity has broken itself against the laws of Nature. As far as we are able to attain conformity to those laws, we find ourselves happy, well, and free. Every glimpse we have into the right adjustment of natural laws discloses a heavenly beauty translated to the earth. Natural laws are God's work, right and kind, the best for man in his present state of being. Is not, then, God's way most godlike? He cannot break down His glorious laws to suit the perverted needs of the fallen race; but by redemption and by consolation He would bring up the fallen race to know that there is hope of recovering, here in part, hereafter absolutely, the Divine order. If God suspended natural laws so that sin and misuse no longer wrought out their consequences to the bitter end, upon the innocent as well as upon the guilty, what a blow would thus be dealt at the moral nature of man! Even now he sins, knowing often by the brightest light of knowledge, that the wages of his sin is death, and that the sting of death is sin. But what would man's moral life become, what would the corruption of society become, if God, ignoring His own law: "Whatsoever a man soweth, that shall he also reap;" a law which operates as much for happiness as it does for misery; should tempt man, as the Devil tempts him, with the hope of escape from the natural consequences of sin: "Thou shalt not surely die."

When our hearts are sorely suffering with beholding the pains of some loved one; when the inexorable laws of Nature are grinding the life out of some dear form that we would not touch save with the touch of blessing and the kiss of peace, although we may not believe that awful paganism that God is the direct sender of this suffering, although our minds may be enlightened so far as to know that sickness and agony and death occur not because of God's laws, but because of humanity's sad misadjustment to those laws through the world's long generations of sin, still comes there not unbidden the passionate longing that God would for our sake suspend those laws, and stop those inexorable wheels that grind away at the precious life. And when the wheels go on still and finish their work, has there not been in many a heart the embittered doubt of the love of Him of Whom we dare to say: "He could have stopped those wheels if He would"? Ah! we wrong Him, we wrong Him by that thought; we wrong the love of Him Who put

Himself under those very wheels, and let Himself be ground to death. Have we the right to believe that He loves *our* loved one only, and loves not also every single one of His poor, suffering children? Have we the right to believe He would wish to help us only and not also to help *all?* But what would it be to help all? What would it mean for God to prevent all suffering, to stay all the forces that are at work, making misery for Humanity; what would it mean for God to keep those effects from following their legitimate causes, which bring heaviness to the heart, weariness to the frame, tears on the cheeks, fever in the blood? It would be to overturn the laws of Nature, it would be to bring anarchy into that system of order, which, however men may misuse it, and sin against it, and break themselves to pieces on its marble solidity, is still the best for the individual and for the race, still the only vestige of the divine order remaining in the earth; it would be to make life intolerable, to throw all human plans, efforts, and calculations into chaos, to upheave the very world, and send the whole human system of things staggering into hopeless confusion, as a ship on her beam-ends in a cyclonic sea. No! as long as it is necessary for the present state of being to continue, it is necessary for the laws of nature to do their work, inexorably blessing, inexorably blasting. Man has undone himself and his children in God's fair universe, and the heart of God is sorry for Him, with a divine pity and pain. And the consolations of God are poured out upon him through the Christ his Redeemer, and the Word his Gospel, and the Spirit his Comforter. And as the complications under natural law grow worse and worse, as the innocent reap what the guilty have sown, and the Nemesis of physical retribution follows the scent of physical wrong-doing, as the pathos of creation intensifies, and the vast procession to the tomb is augmented by the world's increasing populations, God Himself tells us that the sorrows of the race lie upon His heart, and that He is hastening on the new dispensation. The laws of the present natural order cannot be unhinged and set aside at the pleasure of a million contradictory desires. For the good of all, the order must go on to its consummation. But He Who died in the earth is risen to the heavens, whence He shall come to bring in a new day of hope. And there is meaning in that prayer: "Thy Kingdom come, Thy Will be done, in earth as it is in heaven." We do not look for the suspension of laws and for the elimination of pain in the present order. But we look for "a new heaven and a new earth, wherein dwelleth righteousness; when the tabernacle of God shall be with men, and He shall dwell with them and they shall be His peoples; and God Himself shall be with them and be their God; when He shall wipe away every tear from their eyes, and death shall be no more; neither shall there be mourning, nor crying, nor pain any more, for the first things shall have passed away." Thus is God related to natural law. He is the Author of order, of harmony, of beauty; and the disorder, the discord, the disfigurement, the disintegration of the race under natural laws, are the fruits of man's misuse of laws, not the work of God nor of His laws.

Concerning God's relation to *chastisement*, the New Testament suggests these familiar words: "Whom the Lord loveth He chasteneth." By a great misfortune in the association of ideas, chastisement is understood by many to mean "punishment." "To chastise" does to the modern ear mean bodily punishment. Hence we hear constantly in our conventional religious speech of chastisements and punishments coming from the hand of God upon men, both upon Christians and upon unbelievers;

and the world is full of events transpiring in the private and public walks of life which are described as chastisements visited by God upon men for their offenses. A man who has lived a proud, dissolute, worldly life is smitten with a disease which makes him a burden to himself and to his friends; or a household which has grown worldly has one of its fair children snatched away by sudden death. We are told conventionally that this is God's chastisement upon these worldly people for their sins. And out of this mode of speech grows vast self-righteousness, not to say vast impertinence, whereby one man presumes to affirm that another has been visited with special punishment from the Most High. Is there any ground in the New Testament for affirming that God ever punishes men with physical or material calamities in the present life? None whatever. "Punishment" is a word never used in the New Testament to describe God's dealings with men in the present life. Christ repudiates the idea of physical retribution in this life. We read in St. Luke: "There were some present which told Him of the Galileans whose blood Pilate had mingled with their sacrifices." The Lord's answer clearly shows that this incident was pointed out to Him as an example of punishment for sin. He answered and said: "Think ye that these Galileans were sinners above all the Galileans because they have suffered these things? I tell you, nay, but except ye repent ye shall all in like manner perish. Or those eighteen," He continues, "upon whom the tower in Siloam fell, and killed them, think ye that they were offenders above all the men that dwell in Jerusalem? I tell you, nay, but except ye repent ye shall all likewise perish." The civil law punishes men, or some men, for their sins in this life. God does not. If a bad man breaks natural laws, he will suffer; but not because he is a bad man. If a good man breaks natural laws, he will suffer just as much as if he were bad. If a child is snatched away from a worldly family by sudden death, it is not because the family is worldly, but because the child caught the prevailing fever. Perhaps it caught it from the little child next door, who belonged to a most holy and devout family, and who also caught the fever and died. Side by side in their beds, side by side in their graves, lie the dear little children; two homes in mourning, yet neither one family nor the other is being punished for its sin. God is not punishing now. He is saving, with every possible effort of His loving heart. Into this world

Christ has come, not to condemn the world, but that the world through Him may be saved. The whole subject of punishment is reserved for the future dispensations. Now is the accepted time, now is the day of salvation. Later on, in a future dispensation, those who refuse the Love of God, who trample under foot the Son of God, who despise the Spirit of God, must reckon with God for what they have chosen to do. I know not how, I dare not say, nor imagine, how they will reckon with Him or He with them; but now there is not punishment. Sickness is not judgment, death is not retribution; they are purely natural phenomena issuing from causes more or less traceable. Let my tongue cleave to the roof of my mouth before I, a sinner, dare to say of other sinners weeping by their dead, " God is punishing them for their sins." To-morrow I may be weeping by my dead — and what then?

But how shall we adjust with these views the fact of chastisements of which undoubtedly the New Testament speaks? Very readily, by observing that chastisement is not punishment for sin, but a spiritual process of purification from sin. Chastisement is "to make chaste," and "chaste" is the beautiful, snowy, Latin "castus," spotless, pure, holy. Study every passage in the New Testament referring to God's chastisements, and you will not find one connected with physical calamities and sorrows. The connection is wholly spiritual. "Chastisement" is the office of the Spirit. Whatever gracious work of the Spirit quickens within one the consciousness and conviction of sin, is chastisement. Whatever brings in upon us the self-humiliations and rebukings that spring from our wounding of Jesus through our sins, is chastisement. Whatever pain of our spirit thrills us in the presence of our suffering Lord, so that the scourges that fell on Him bite the very flesh of our souls; whatever "via crucis" opens at the beckoning of His hand, leading us on till we have crucified with Him unsanctified passions or unfaithful fears, and have come on, as through the solemn fellowship of His grave, into the buoyant and blessed communion of His risen life; whatever holy chalice of His grace comes to our lips, tasting of which we spring renewed into loftier living, casting off the works of darkness, girding on with brave hands the gleaming armor of light — *that* is chastisement, a work of the Spirit, making the soul chaste, white, and knightly for the kingdom of God.

What is the relation of God to *discipline?*

No intelligent answer can be given until we
realize that discipline, as well as chastisement,
is not punishment for sin. Discipline is the
education of the disciple—"discere," *to learn.*
" The disciple," says the Great Head Master of
the School of Grace, "is not above his Teacher.
It is enough for the disciple that he be as his
Teacher." Chastisement is the purifying of
man's spirit. Discipline is the education of
man's spirit. The end in both cases is the same,
the one consummate end for every human life,
the end which the loving Father purposed for
us from the foundation of the world, that we
should be conformed to the image of His Son;
that we should be like Christ, like Christ in
purity, like Christ in power. Chastisement is
the purifying office of grace, making our spirits
chaste. Discipline is the educating office of
grace, making our spirits calm and strong and
faithful and patient and mighty for usefulness. To assist Him in this process of education our teacher uses everything good, evil,
bright, dark, joyous, painful, that comes into
our life in the natural order of events. Through
every hardship that develops from the distor-
tions of the natural order, He seeks to throw
into our minds some magnificent suggestion of
patience, valor, and victory; through every

pang of physical suffering, as well as through every thrill of physical health, He, mightiest of teachers, works or seeks to work some broadening influence of grace; through the dark mists of death, that last and most awful catastrophe of our shattered life, He, most faithful of friends, still reaches us with His glorious teaching, till again and again, the disciple, neither seduced by life's pleasure nor vanquished by life's woe, grows up, through the discipline of years, toward the measure of the stature of Christ, and becomes like his Teacher. Christ is indeed everything to those who believe this — "Christus Salvator," Saviour of our lives; "Christus Consolator," God's great Answer of love to His bruised and suffering creation; "Christus Doctor," Christ the Teacher, training the disciple upward to grander living, lightening all our darkness, broadening all our narrowness, and flooding our path with the dear fulfillments of His own promise: "I am the Light of the World. He that followeth Me shall not walk in darkness, but shall have the Light of Life."

CHAPTER III.

THE HISTORIC ATONEMENT AND THE PUNISHMENT OF SIN.

We have an Advocate with the Father, Jesus Christ the Righteous, and He is the Propitiation for our sins, and not for ours only, but also for the whole world. — 1 EPISTLE OF ST. JOHN. (Revised Version.)

God was in Christ, reconciling the world unto Himself, not reckoning unto them their trespasses, and having committed unto us the ministry of reconciliation. — 2 EPISTLE TO THE CORINTHIANS. (Revised Version.)

While we were enemies, we were reconciled to God through the death of His Son. — EPISTLE TO THE ROMANS.

Now is the accepted time, now is the day of salvation. — 2 EPISTLE TO THE CORINTHIANS.

CHAPTER III.

THE HISTORIC ATONEMENT AND THE PUNISHMENT OF SIN.

My objective point in this teaching has from the beginning been this: To show that God is Love, although the world be full of sin, of sorrow, and of death; to show that the Eternal God is not our tormentor, but our Refuge, to Whom, in the woes of life and death, we run to hide ourselves, and in the embrace of Whose Everlasting Arms we shall be sustained until these calamities are overpast. In the process of this teaching we have had occasion to examine the relation of God to Natural Law, to Chastisement, and to Discipline. As to natural laws, those lines of order running out through the whole creation, we have seen that they are made for man, and that he was made in perfect adaptation to them, so that they are the best for him as God made him. We have seen that sin is man's misadjustment to law: in sin man has related himself adversely to law, thereby causing sorrow and sickness and every variety of trouble — even death itself — to spread like a pall over the earth. We have seen that although miracles show us that God has power to interpose in the working of laws, and so to recombine them as to produce results the reverse of those for which experience has taught us to look, yet our reason tells us that, for the good of all, the reign of law must continue as long as this present order continues. If God should intervene, as sometimes we blindly seem to think He ought to intervene, for the purpose of putting a stop to human suffering, it would mean the suspension of natural laws and the throwing into confusion of our present system of life, which, in all its calculations and efforts, depends on the changelessness of laws. Our conclusion, therefore, concerning the manifold sufferings, sorrows, sicknesses, and deaths which transpire in the world under natural law, is this: that they are not punishments from God, sent in retribution upon man for his sins, but that they are the natural and inevitable consequences of man's own sins, working themselves out through the sequence of cause and effect, perhaps through generations of persons innocent of all other connection with the original act of wrong save that of involuntary inheritance; they are the consequences, occurring under processes of natural law, of man's innumerable bodily or mental perversions of law, man's innumerable *wrong uses of right things*. From Natural Law we proceeded to speak of those two ideas which the New Testament presents as undoubted elements of God's dealings with His children, viz.: *Chastisement* and *Discipline;* and of those we saw that neither chastisement nor discipline is punishment, according to the New Testament; that chastisement and discipline are offices of the Holy Spirit, — the one the purifying or making chaste of our spirit, the other the educating or training of our spirit; that the idea of punishment for sin does not enter into chastisement, but instead the spiritual work of purifying the inner life from sin; and that the idea of punishment for sin does not enter into discipline, but wholly a gracious teaching and guiding and elevating of our spirit by a work of grace which may make use of any and every incident and element of our daily life as an instrument, even a sacrament, through which to broaden or uplift our views of life and of God, that the disciple may become like His Teacher. These views, although in no sense original with the writer, doubtless come to some as new views, as views which have not hitherto been entertained among Christians. And certainly these views of chastisement and discipline, as purely and entirely works of spiritual purification and education, differ from other views which hold that God is now punishing men for their sins through physical or financial adversities; that sickness is often sent to us as a sharp rebuke for some proud or unfilial attitude toward God, and that death comes sometimes into a family as a punishment for worldliness, or smites directly an evil-doer in the sinful act, even as Ananias and Sapphira were miraculously smitten at a time in the history of the Church when miracles were needed for the accrediting and enforcement of a new dispensation. Now, if these teachings which we have expressed concerning the nature of chastisement and discipline, as being absolutely without punishment, involved no important conclusions, it might not be worth while to dwell upon them further; it might be more expedient to pass them by as opinions of an individual entitled to no special consideration. But to those to whom these teachings are new, they involve such wide departures from the opinions which hold that God is punishing people now for their sins, and they suggest conclusions so apparently startling, not to say revolutionary, concerning the nature of suffering and death, that it becomes an all-important duty to state the ground upon which we maintain our position.

I now proceed to state that ground in three words: *The Historic Atonement.* " He is the propitiation for our sins, and not for ours only, but also for the whole world." " God was in Christ, reconciling the world unto Himself, not reckoning unto them their trespasses, and having committed unto us the word of reconciliation." " While we were enemies, we were reconciled to God through the death of His Son."

In speaking now of the meaning of the death of Christ, I have no desire to state a " theory of the Atonement." I believe the Atonement is something far greater than man ever has or ever can put into words. How many systems of theology have fought their battles at the Cross, each system, it may be, containing some measure of the truth, but not one containing all the truth! But we may escape all these controversies of theology, and think simply and plainly upon the meaning of Christ's death.

Let us think of the death of Christ as the *historic* Atonement, an event in time. Sometimes the whole thought of the Incarnation of the Son of God, of His relation to Humanity, opens out before the mind in such enormous expanse, presents to the intellect such vast problems, and leads to such stupendous conclusions, it is almost impossible to realize its successive stages as actual historic events: the Annunciation, the Nativity, the Baptism, the Temptation, the Passion, the Death, the Burial, the Resurrection, the Ascension. Yet if we hold them at all, we must hold them as historic events. We must know them as facts in the order of time; must admit that if it were possible for us to walk back through the long valley of the receding centuries we would come at last to "the green hill far away," by that great city's wall; we would be swallowed up in that surging crowd and swept upon its raging bosom up, up, up, to the foot of the Cross. Yes, it is real. More and more I am realizing the Crucifixion of the Son of God as an event which I might have been called to witness with my own eyes had I but been born earlier in the history of the world.

And let us think of the death of Christ not only as historic, but as the historic *Atonement*. The "theories of the Atonement," as they are called, are hard to understand, and very often they fail to satisfy when understood. But the fact is as simple as the outline of the Cross. The dear Lord Jesus is laying down His life for the life of the world. We may not know, we cannot tell what pains He had to bear; we may not know, we cannot tell what awful necessity in the holiness of God's life was fulfilled by the obedient and willing sufferings of Our Lord; we may not know, we cannot tell the answers to many, many thoughts which arise in our minds around the historic Atonement. But our faith is very simple and very clear: "We believe it was for us He hung and suffered there;" we believe that on the shoulders of Our Blessed Jesus rested the punishment for the sin of the world. "Behold the Lamb of God which beareth the sin of the world." "He was wounded for our transgressions; He was bruised for our iniquities; the chastisement of our peace was upon Him, and by His stripes we are healed. And Jehovah hath laid on Him the iniquity of us all." This is the relation of the death of Christ to the sin, not of a few, not of a class, not of a nation, not of an age, but to the sin of the world as such, to sin as the great sad fact in Humanity's life. We have seen, in the earlier parts of this process of thought, what the nature of sin is, that it is *lawlessness*, it is man's putting himself in wrong relations to God's laws. We have seen that the natural consequences of these terrible and constant wrong uses of right laws through all the generations of time have been the accumulated miseries, sorrows, sicknesses, poverties, and deaths of earth; and we have seen that those consequences produced by man's own imprudences and evil choices cannot be suspended in the present order; to suspend them in the present order would be to upset the order itself, and therefore the sorrows and tribulations caused by sin must go on, except as by skill or care or holy living they are alleviated in individual cases. But the death of Christ brings into view another terrible fact about sin altogether beyond that fact of the sad natural consequences with which experience has made us familiar. That additional fact, brought into view by the death of Christ, is the fact that sin is not only sorrow to man, but wrong to God, a crime against His holiness which *must* be punished. The punishment for sin as a crime against God is something entirely beyond and above what we mean by the natural consequences of sin. The natural consequences of sin, under the operation of natural laws, we see all about us in the thousand sorrows and ills of life. But when we talk of punishment, of retribution for sin, as visited from God through that necessity of His Holy Being which compels Him to vindicate His nature against wrong, do not let us belittle the same by speaking of earthly events as *punishment*. There is but one place on earth where man obtains a glimpse of what the punishment of sin is as a crime against God. That place is the Hill of Calvary, where stands the Cross of Jesus Christ. When we can look into the secret anguish of that sacred heart; when we can comprehend the horror and misery that rent His soul; when we can understand the hideous sense of alienation from all good which surged over Him in that frightful darkness, wringing from His lips the shriek, "*Forsaken;*" when we can rise to the point of grasping that, — then, and not till then, may we think that we comprehend what the *punishment of sin* is. The punishment of sin! God knows what it is, and to His mind it is something so awful, His one purpose from the foundation of the world has been to redeem the world from that doom. And He has redeemed the world, the whole world, every creature in the world, from that saddest of fates. God so loved the world, He gave His Only Begotten

Son, that whosoever believeth in Him should not perish, but have everlasting life. Christ has suffered punishment; He has been into that black mystery; He has gone to the bottom of it. And when I think of the nameless horror of His punishment, the only uninspired language which approaches a description of it is that clause in the creed (which some tell us we ought to reject as unscriptural), *"He descended into hell."* I cannot reject these words from the creed. Ah! When that shriek, "*Forsaken,*" burst from the pallid lips of Jesus Christ, was He not descending into hell?

"Yea, once, Immanuel's orphaned cry His universe hath shaken.
It went up, single, echoless, 'My God! I am forsaken!'
It went up from the Holy's Lips amid His lost creation,
That, of the lost, no son should use those words of desolation."

If this is true, if sin is such a wounding of God's life that the punishment of sin required Christ's death; if the Beloved Son came forth from the bosom of the Father to be a Propitiation for our sins, and not for ours only, but also for the whole world; if God was in Christ in that supreme tragedy of the Cross, reconciling the world unto Himself, and not reckoning unto them their trespasses, but piling them, a crushing weight, on the bleeding heart of Jesus; if that holy sacrifice was indeed made *for all*, and once for all, then three conclusions appear to be established, conclusions bearing very closely and forcibly upon the teachings contained in the foregoing chapters.

The first conclusion relates to God's present attitude toward the world in the dispensation of the Gospel. It is an attitude of perfect love. God has redeemed the world; but not from the natural consequences of sin: those have involved the life of every individual, and have so comprehensively affected the race that to suspend them would bring the whole system of natural laws into instant collapse. Redemption from these natural consequences is impossible; the consequences go on, and what is sown, that must be reaped. From what, then, has He redeemed the world? From that which is too terrible for man to imagine: the punishment which comes, not out of natural law, but out of God's holy life, upon sin, by the very necessity of His being. This has been borne once for all Humanity by the Incarnate Son of God. We cannot describe it. We do not know what it is. Christ has been through it, and that cry of His, "Forsaken," is the only clue we have, to tell us what it is. But from the hour that cry sounded, the world was redeemed; every creature in the world was redeemed. The whole relation of the world was changed: it was reconciled unto Himself. Before that suffering there was nothing in store for the world but that nameless horror; but by that suffering the horror is lifted from Humanity for all save those who finally and forever reject Christ. Let us not confuse the revelation of God's love by attempting to pronounce on the destiny of those who have entered and have left the world in ignorance of Christ and of His Sacrifice. We may safely trust Him with them, and trust them to Him. And whatever we may affirm or deny concerning them, our faith has nailed this inscription on the Cross, written not in three languages, but in every language spoken among men: "He is the Propitiation for our sins, and not for ours only, but also for the whole world."

The second conclusion which we reach relates to the teaching that chastisement and discipline are not God's punishments for sins; that sickness and death and sorrow are not God's punishments for sin; that God is not punishing any one in the world. I believe that sin has been judged, condemned, and punished in this world, once for all, in the awful sacrifice of Jesus Christ. I believe that that sacrifice of the Cross is the one divine event toward which the whole creation moves. Prophecy looked forward to it with longing expectations. Faith looks back to it with absolute confidence. Then and there, in Him, punishment was endured, not for our sins only, but also for the whole world. And it is only because I believe this, I can preach the Gospel, can say to every creature in the world, Jesus Christ has suffered for you; Jesus Christ has borne your punishment; you are free. How, then, can we believe that God is now engaged in punishing us for our sins? To believe this discredits the Atonement. To believe that God punishes any one for sin now is to bring the charge of insincerity against His Love, and the charge of insufficiency against the historic Atonement. Natural laws work out their own retributions on those who break them, but God's punishment of sin has been borne for the world on Calvary.

The last conclusion can be stated in a word. It relates to the fate of those who finally and forever reject Jesus Christ. If any soul were finally and forever to put Jesus Christ aside (and on this side of the grave it is impossible for us to understand what that may mean, or to know what dealings with Christ souls may have hereafter), but, if any soul were finally and forever to put aside Him Who has vicariously borne the punishment of sin, it must bear its own punishment, for it places itself under those conditions which brought from Christ's lips the cry "FORSAKEN." We have only one Saviour. His sufferings have redeemed the world. If we put Him aside, there is no other to rise up and take His place. The alternative is this: to meet the future alone, because *forsaken*, or to be saved in Him, Who was "forsaken" that all men might be forgiven; Who descended into hell that all men might ascend into heaven; Who was separated in darkness from His Father's face that all men might behold that face in righteousness and peace forever and ever.

CHAPTER IV.

THE WILL OF GOD AND THE TENDENCY OF NATURE.

Thy Will be done. — GOSPEL OF ST. MATTHEW.

Be ye not unwise, but understanding what the will of the Lord is. — EPISTLE TO THE EPHESIANS.

CHAPTER IV.

THE WILL OF GOD AND THE TENDENCY OF NATURE.

THE common speech of Christians contains many unconscious perversions of the plain sense of Scripture. Many phrases of the Word of God have been broken away from their environment, and have been handed down through devotional literature and through pulpit use in forced association with unscriptural ideas. These misapplied phrases, sanctioned by common consent, have given a disastrous force to opinions and beliefs not in accordance with New Testament truth. It is not an enviable task to raise one's voice against these venerable perversions of Scripture. Nevertheless, he who does it may thereby serve the truth. Hardly any words in the whole vocabulary of religion are so widely, so continually, so painfully misunderstood and misapplied as the blessed words: "Thy will be done." Never were words, meant to comfort, so turned into an instrument of needless torture as those words: "Thy will be done." Never were words, meant to cheer and to nourish faith, so perverted into the stumbling-block of faith as those words, "Thy will be done." Never were words, meant to magnify God's love, so distorted into a gospel of cruelty as those words, "Thy will be done." By what process of perversion they were first broken away from their proper environment of thought and made the basis of what has been to myriads a doctrine of despair, I cannot here undertake to say. By what chain of historic and dogmatic influences they have attained their almost universal dominion over the Christian consciousness, I may not attempt to tell. But one thing must not be left unsaid, that when we enumerate the forces which have contributed most fruitfully to the sorrows of the human heart, we must name among the more powerful of those forces the misdirected words, "Thy will be done."

He who goes much among the suffering sons and daughters of men, especially among those who are sick, or whose loved ones are sick, dying, or dead, will find, ere he has gone far, two classes of persons whose condition verifies all that has been said: the silently despondent, the openly rebellious. Here sits a mother, empty-handed, broken-hearted. There, on the little bed, all too smoothly folded, is the alabaster face that never more shall flush with joy, set round with curls that never more shall toss with play. Still, cold, white — mother and child alike. All is over, and now for the child, its suffering done, its paradise regained — the death of sorrow; for the mother, her suffering only begun, and lonely life before her — the sorrow of death. For now she is trying to do the thing her reason rejects, while her religion (as she thinks) commands to say, "Thy will be done." She is trying to make herself believe that God's blessed will has broken her heart, and that it is good and kind in killing her child. Poor soul! as if death were not enough, she must attempt the torture of worshiping Death, the last enemy, as the will of God. And this also one sees, among the suffering: the heart which, chained by tradition to that terrible creed that sickness and death are God's will for His children, takes the only revenge upon God left within its reach to take — the revenge of rebellion. Breaking away from the hand which, as it believes, has dealt the cruel, shattering blow, it cries out in its pain words of rejection, words of rebellion, words of helpless hatred which I have heard too often ever to forget.

It is the deep-seated, almost the universal belief, — fostered, alas, by the holiest doctrines of our religion; taught, alas, with the purest and best motives; illustrated, alas, in the lives of some of the saintliest ones who have ever walked as Christ's servants on the earth, — that the physical sufferings of man are the will of God; that Christian character requires us to look upon the pangs of the body in ourselves and in others, and upon the misery of bereavement, as the mysterious portion which God wills for us; that when our friends succumb to disease, and pass away under the processes of natural law, we must, as Christians, adopt for ourselves that Old Testament saying of Eli (which he used only in that horrible moment when the sentence of judgment and retribution was passed upon his impious sons, for the most vile profanations of the house of God), "It is the Lord, let Him do what seemeth Him good." As though sickness were not of itself sufficiently repulsive, sufficiently suggestive of a broken-down order of nature; as though death, no matter how with the gentler modes of our advanced civilization we attempt to idealize it by covering it with flowers, by concealing its ghastly accessories, and by clothing our very speech with beautiful and noble metaphors, — as though death, I say, were not the same dreadful and hopeless catastrophe wherever we meet it, — on the battlefield, in the railway accident, on the sinking ship, or in the beloved home surrounded by comfort and love, — an almost universal tradition, appropriating and distorting the very words of the Saviour, has succeeded in making most people share in the general attempt of self-delusion, to wit, that these last terrors of humanity, these cloven rocks from which have gushed the tears of ages, were stricken open by God's hand, and are indeed the very will of Him Whom we are told that we must love with all our soul and with all our heart and with all our mind and with all our strength.

This attempt to persuade ourselves that it is God's will that we suffer and die, and all the consequent efforts of religious philosophy to reconcile a God of love with a will so terrific, have proceeded from a twofold cause, from a desire to honor the providence of God, and from a misuse of Christian Scripture to support that desire. The desire to honor the providence of God has led men from a beautiful truth to a terrible deduction. The beautiful truth is that not a sparrow falls to the ground without the notice of Our Father; that the very hairs of our head are all numbered; that all things work together for good to them that love God. The terrible deduction for which God's Word gives us no warrant is that therefore every event of our life, not only the greatest blessing, but the greatest catastrophe, comes from our Father's hand, and is an expression of His holy, though often inscrutable will. A deduction which leads to conclusions more horrible than can be fully understood, except by those who have either broken their own hearts or have seen others break their hearts in the effort to accept a will of God which did violence to His character, must, in order to stand, claim the authority of the Divine Word in its defense. And this it has done to an amazing extent by perverting the meanings of Scriptures, which, in their perverted form, have become so ingrained in the speech and in the prose and poetical literature of Christianity, it is next to impossible to convince many that these so-called proof-texts upon the will of God in ordering all physical calamities are not Scripture proofs, but Scripture perversions. For example, passing by the famous passage in Hebrews upon the subject of chastisement, or the purifying of the heart striving against sin, to which I have alluded in a previous chapter, the words in 1 Peter iv. are constantly quoted to show that our physical sufferings are the will of God. "Let them that suffer according to the will of God commit the keeping of their souls to Him." Read the context about the fiery trial, and see that it bears not upon the natural routine of sickness and death, but bears wholly upon the persecutions of Christians by unbelievers, being reproached for the name of Christ. To bear *that* reproach fearlessly *is* to suffer according to the will of God. Recall that famous passage in John xvii., "What I do thou knowest not now, but thou shalt know hereafter." Innumerable times have those words been spoken over the coffin of a child, as if to comfort parents with the thought that God had done this, and that He would interpret His will hereafter. But in the Bible those words have not the slightest relation to suffering of any kind. They are Christ's words to Peter, when Peter, from a mistaken impulse, refused to permit Christ to bathe the Apostle's feet. Take once more those terrible whispers of grief which fell from the Saviour's lips in the silent darkness of Gethsemane: "Oh! My Father, if it be possible, let this cup pass from Me; nevertheless, not as I will, but as Thou wilt. The cup which

My Father hath given Me, shall I not drink it?" Words are those so tremendous in their relation to the sacrifice of which I have already spoken — that historic Atonement just about to be offered; words so intimately associated with the anguish of Christ's heart on entering His unique sufferings, — it sometimes seems to me almost a presumptuous intrusion upon the grief of Christ to repeat those words aloud, much less to apply them in any sense to ourselves. Let us not forget *what* that cup was which the Father was offering to the lips of the Redeemer. Let us not forget that the obedient Son, once for all, accepted that cup of punishment on behalf of Humanity. Let us not take language divinely unique, and make it our commonplace. And especially when we remember what we are told of the origin of sickness and death (as for example, in Heb. ii., that he who has the power of death is *not* the Father, but the *devil*), let us not seek a perverted comfort in bereavement by saying : " The cup which my *Father* hath given me, shall I not drink it?" And yet once more: "Thy will be done!" That petition from the Lord's Prayer is the classic proof-text of the doctrine that when our hearts are broken with sorrow; when the desire of our eyes has been tortured

and put to death; when misery has crushed
the brave wife, and she gathers her frightened
little children around her, and tells them they
are orphans and penniless, she must force herself to believe, and must force *them* to believe
that this cruel wreck is the will of Him Who
calls Himself by the name of Love. Yet this
is no proof-text, but a perversion of the plain
sense of Scripture; it is tradition's clumsy
hand tearing a glorious sentence out of its
environment, and using it for a purpose never
contemplated by its Author. "Thy will be
done." What has that to do with sickness
and death in this world? Much verily; but
not that which many have been taught to believe, that sickness is the will, and death the
will of God, to which we are to submit as
sent from Him. Just the opposite to that is
what Christ taught us to pray: "Thy kingdom come. Thy will be done in earth, *as
it is in heaven.*" Yes, as it is in heaven,
where the blessed order of peace is not in-
vaded by death and the sting of death, which
is sin; in heaven, where no such catastrophe
has entered as that which has turned this world
upside down, and has brought to confusion
God's beautiful order of life, perverting kind
laws till they become instruments of ruin to

the race which perverts them. Christ has taught us to pray for the hastening of a new dispensation, for the passing away of this broken order in which the will of God is not done, in which sickness and death are constant protests against His will, and for the coming in of the new heavens and the new earth, glorious with the kingship of Jesus realized upon it; an earth in which there shall be no more death, nor pain, nor sorrow, nor crying, no more of anything contrary to our Father's loving will; an earth in which His will shall be done as it is in heaven.

Before venturing on the utterance of these words concerning *the Will of God and the Tendency of Nature*, I have laboriously and freshly examined every single passage in the New Testament bearing upon the subject of God's will, and I have also examined freshly every single passage in the New Testament bearing upon suffering and affliction. I fail to find one which warrants the belief that sickness and death are the will of God, sent directly by His hand upon us. And if the New Testament revelation fails to support that opinion which has taught us to look on sickness or on death as the direct sendings from God, does not our reason rise up with unanswerable arguments to support the contrary conclusion? If sickness and death are God's will, things He sends upon us for our good, what right have we to resist death, or to fight those brave fights against sickness which are going forward to-day on and around so many a sick-bed? Tradition tells us when our child is stricken down with deadly disease, we must accept the visitation as God's will, and bow submissively to it. By what right, then, do we send for the doctor and the nurse, and implore them to do all that skill and faithfulness can accomplish for the recovery of this loved one? What are we doing? Are we fighting against God? Are we trying to outwit the will of God with hot-baths and fever powders? If this is God's will, we ought to promote it, to fan the fever-fire, to help the pneumonia, and to pray as we hurry our darlings to their graves, "Thy will be done." If sickness and suffering are according to the will of God, then every physician is a law-breaker; every trained nurse is defying the Almighty; every hospital is a house of rebellion instead of a house of mercy, and all those conditions which increase suffering and breed sickness are fulfillments of the will of God, and sanitation is blasphemy. This tradition quickly reasons itself out into impossibility.

The only absolutely logical holders of it are those who, accepting sickness as God's will, refuse to employ medical aid for their sick children; and the civil law has now made that refusal a crime. Why, then, in a vain effort of reverence and devotion toward God, do we persist in claiming events to be the will of God, against the consummation of which events the most religious do not hesitate to fight with every resource of wealth and skill? Why does a devoutly Christian father, whose daughter is consumptive, declare with apparent sincerity that that disease is God's will for his child, when, at the very moment of that declaration he is spending a fortune to take that child to the Riviera, to Algiers, anywhere on God's earth, in the hope of conquering the disease? Is he trying to outwit God? No, he says he is not. What, then, is he doing? When that saddest of tragedies occurred in England, and a loving wife, seeking to ease the sufferings of her husband, lifted by mistake the wrong vial, and administered with her own hand a potion that sent into swift unconsciousness and death one of the greatest thinkers of this century, was it her duty to say, "It is the will of God"? Had she administered that fatal dose of chloral intentionally, as a murderess, I think we would hesitate to say that she did it by the will of God. Why, then, should we say so when she does it by mistake? When one of the young collegians who have lately taken part with insane desperation in what was once a noble game, and what may yet be brought back to be a noble game (but has now gathered about itself an atmosphere of brutality and debauchery against which it is the duty of all collegians and non-collegians to protest), when one of these young men shall in a few years develop, to the grief of his heartbroken parents, that peculiar form of tuberculosis which I am told by medical men is likely to result from these irrational exertions, shall those parents or shall their helpless son be taught that they must look to that Father above, Who will then be their only refuge, and must believe that He has sent this deadly blow to all their hopes? But I have pursued this subject sufficiently far. And if in so doing I have said aught which has seemed unjust to the beliefs of any, I ask forgiveness for those words. They were not spoken except in tenderness of purpose. It seems to me that one would almost be willing to lay down one's life, feeling that it could not be more complete, if one might be the means of lifting from the heart of man the burden which he has so long borne in his attempt to see in sickness and in death, not the perpetual catastrophe of a natural order perverted through sin, not a state of things contrary to the divine order, but a dispensation, a sending, an ordering of the Heavenly Father — a bitter, revolting cup pressed to the unwilling lips of man by the unsparing hand of God.

But I seem to hear the question asked in doubtful hearts: What, then, becomes of that thought, so precious to a Christian, of doing God's will? Are we no longer to say: "Thy will be done"? Must those great words be laid aside? God forbid! How could they be laid aside when Christ holds them out to us as the very end and substance of all living? "My meat is to do the will of Him that sent Me, and whosoever doeth the will of My Father that is in heaven, the same is My brother and sister and mother." How could they be laid aside in the face of that mighty outburst of apostolic witness to the blessedness of doing the will of God? "That ye may prove," says St. Paul, "what is that good and acceptable and perfect will of God." "That ye may be filled with the knowledge of His will." "That ye may stand perfect and complete in all the will of

God." "He that doeth the will of God," says St. John, "abideth forever." The constant prayer of a Christian cannot be other than this: "Thy will be done, for me, by me, in me, through me." This prayer becomes both more intelligent and more intense as he realizes that for the present he is placed in an order where many forces, physical, intellectual, spiritual, are warring against the will of God. In the midst of these forces warring against God's will, forces which attack the body, the mind, and the spirit, the Christian feels that he is set, that the true will of God may be done by him, and may be shown forth to the world in him. And so, standing between the blessed love of God on the one hand, and on the other hand the fierce, discordant elements of sin and pain and sickness and death which fill the world, to him, "Thy will be done," means three things: it means the fellowship of Christ's sufferings; it means the manifestation of the grace of God; it means the courage of faith.

"*Thy will be done.*" *It means the fellowship of Christ's sufferings.* He remembers that Jesus Christ came down into this world, and bore the brunt of its warring elements. Him the Devil tempted; Him the storm of sorrow struck shelterless; Him bodily pain wrenched and bruised; Him death had dominion over for a season; and the motive of it all was pure and utter love, devotion to the souls and bodies of men. All this the Christian remembers; and then he thinks that he himself is in the same world where Christ suffered, amidst the same warring elements of pain and death that swept over the body of Christ. And because Christ came into the midst of all these dreadful storms and hardships, so contrary to the Father's will, so utterly the fruits of sin and evil, and met them grandly, endured them sweetly, inasmuch as the Father's will was that even in the midst of these deadly things, He, the Son of God, should raise up a mighty salvation; the Christian hopes that he, being set in the midst of the same deadly evils and sorrows, may bear them in a spirit so Christly as that the dear Lord in His glory shall count even the man in his sufferings, the woman in hers, the child in its early woes, a brother, a sister, in the fellowship of the Cross.

"*Thy will be done.*" *It means the manifestation of the grace of God.* The Christian may without presumption look upon himself as a teacher, an interpreter of the grace of God. The whole world is sharing with him the sorrows of life; and he that hath the power of death, that is, the Devil, is doing his utmost through sickness and a weary chain of calamities to drive man to despair. But the Christian has what the world knoweth not: the benediction of the grace of God. This has God shown him that he might show it to others: he can best show its power to others by showing its power in himself. Therefore, with holy pride he seeks so to live in the fellowship of God's will, which is his sanctification, that he shall never fail under any temptation, nor sink into despair under any affliction. And when those fierce temptations of the Devil press him, bodily anguish in himself, or the sight of bodily anguish in those he loves but cannot relieve, then he prays more intensely, "Thy will be done in me! Yea, Lord, let the sweet purpose of Thy grace be accomplished in my strengthening and sanctifying, that even in these devilish temptations of pain and death I may not fail to show to men the reality of the love and the peace and the strength of God."

"*Thy will be done.*" *It means the courage of faith.* He is a servant of Christ, and as such he must go forward, however difficult or painful the path may be made by natural fatigues or by those who oppose the truth. Thus went onward the martyrs of old, meeting pain and death undaunted, because the one thought which made their courage infinite was the ambition that God's glorious will for the world might be carried, even though it were by their sufferings and over their martyred bodies, on toward its triumph. And thus, in humbler ways, yet perchance in the same spirit, we follow them, we who have undertaken anything that is hard, anything that brings strain and toil, and the shortening of our days, for the love of that blessed will of God Who would have all men to be saved and to come unto the knowledge of the truth.

Greatest of all prayers for man on earth, — *Thy Will be done:* sickness and sorrow and death proclaiming everywhere the fierce might of the kingdom of darkness, and we who know the meaning of that prayer, praying and seeking to be as "*light-givers*"[1] in the world, holding forth the Word of Life!

[1] φωστῆρες.

CHAPTER V.

THE DUTY, THE COMFORT, AND THE POWER OF PRAYER.

He spake unto them that men ought always to pray and not to faint. — GOSPEL OF ST. LUKE.

In everything by prayer and supplication, with thanksgiving, let your requests be made known unto God. And the peace of God which passeth all understanding shall guard your hearts and your thoughts in Christ Jesus. — EPISTLE TO THE PHILIPPIANS. (Revised Version.)

Casting all your care upon Him, for He careth for you. — 1 EPISTLE OF ST. PETER.

Is any among you afflicted? Let him pray. — EPISTLE OF ST. JAMES.

CHAPTER V.

THE DUTY, THE COMFORT, AND THE POWER OF PRAYER.

When one undertakes to speak of prayer (a subject concerning which many conflicting opinions exist), one should lose no time in defining the standpoint from which he speaks. The dangers of misunderstanding are, by such frankness, considerably reduced. I therefore state, at the outset, that I speak of prayer from the standpoint of one to whom prayer is (in the language of Montgomery) the Christian's vital breath, the very atmosphere of daily living. I speak from the standpoint of one whose belief in the Duty, the Comfort, and the Power of Prayer is absolute, without mental reservation, full of delight, thankfulness, and experimental appreciation. I regard prayer as a precious and sublime reality, and as one of the most inestimable blessings and one of the most useful endowments which the God of love has given to His children. I believe the realm of prayer is commensurate with life itself; that every interest, great and small, secret and open, joyful and sorrowful, physical, mental, and spiritual, personal, domestic, social, national, universal, falls within the realm of prayer and constitutes legitimate occasion for prayer. I am not aware of language by which to define more clearly the standpoint from which I undertake to speak of prayer.

Among those who have read the foregoing chapters on the relation of God to earthly pain, calamity, and death, there may be some within whom apprehensions have arisen, that the logical conclusion from what has been said would be to disparage the value of prayer and to undermine the faith of those who pray. The current sense of New Testament Scripture upon the subject of prayer is readily ascertained, and what may be said by me upon this subject is not a case of special pleading, resting insecurely on the use of a single text, but is rather, as the preceding argument has been in all its parts, a broad exposition of the current sense of the Christian Scriptures. Four texts may be cited as illustrating that consensus of teaching on this blessed theme which runs through Gospels and Epistles alike, and for each one of the four a score of confirmatory texts might easily be given. From the Gospels we may cite the authority of Christ Himself:

"He spake unto them that men ought always to pray and not to faint." From the Epistles we take the testimony of St. Paul, in a passage of singular comprehensiveness and beauty: "In everything by prayer and supplication, with thanksgiving, let your requests be made known unto God; and the peace of God which passeth all understanding shall guard your hearts and your thoughts in Christ Jesus." We take also the testimony of St. Peter, in words sweeter than any music to our ears: "Casting all your care upon Him, for He careth for you." And we also take the testimony of St. James, in which prayer is directly urged as our refuge in the hour of trouble: "Is any among you afflicted? Let him pray." Beyond these testimonies how easily could we branch through every part of the holy oracles, showing that prayer is as fundamental a conception in the Bible as the idea of God is fundamental.

The thoughts which have occupied our attention thus far upon the relation of God to earthly pain, calamity, and death, having possibly appeared to some readers as involving the disparagement of prayer, it becomes important to inquire upon which portion of these thoughts this apprehension of danger may be founded.

It would probably be founded upon the main proposition: that pain, calamity, sickness, and death are not to be attributed to God as causing them, and as sending them upon us, but that they and all other evils have entered into the world as the fruits and consequences of sin; that man's perverted choices have related him adversely to the laws of God's universe; laws which were framed for a holy race in a holy world, and which would forever have operated blessedly upon a holy race in a holy world, but which are brought violently into collision with the happiness and the life of man through man's own perverted choices. I have sought to impress upon the reader's mind the malignity of evil; to remind him that he that hath the power of death is the Devil; that men born into this disordered world are tempted to relate themselves more and more adversely to natural law, which moving onward, as move it must, through regular processes of cause and effect, scatters calamity, evil, and death everywhere, upon the innocent and guilty without discrimination; the innocent often suffering for the errors of the guilty, and all, both innocent and guilty, yielding at last to the agencies of physical decay, and following the generations of the dead. I have sought to exalt the love of God for man; a love which our sins and failures have never alienated from us; a love which, from the beginning, has held out to man the hope of redemption and restoration; a love which has been historically manifested in Him Who came to bear our griefs and to carry our sorrows, sharing not only by sympathy, but by suffering in our unhappy lot; and which, in the historic Atonement has borne the essential punishment for sin as a Propitiation for the whole world. So that the life which, knowing Christ's love, yet continues in sin; knowing the light, chooses the darkness; knowing the better, chooses the worse; alienates itself from the life of God, and brings at last upon itself that dark and miserable fate which cannot be more fearfully depicted than by the word "Forsaken!" I have sought to impress the thought that, because Christ has suffered once for all in this world the punishment for sin, we ought not to belittle His Atonement or to discredit His sufferings by affirming that our present sufferings and calamities and sicknesses are God's punishments for our sins, or that they are sent upon us by the will of God; but rather that they are fruits and consequences of our fallen estate; that they are all of them opposed to that blessed will which desired and planned for man an existence of Godlike perfection; and that God sorrows with us in all our sorrows, and is our sure Refuge in all our calamities, comforting and purifying us by His grace, and so guiding and teaching our minds by His Spirit that splendid qualities of character may develop in the very midst of adversities, and Christ may be glorified by our fellowship with His sufferings, and by our exhibition in ourselves of the power of God's grace to make us conquerors and more than conquerors in any and every sorrow.

I will assume that these thoughts are by some looked upon with apprehension, lest they disparage prayer. "If it be true," says the objector, "that sickness, calamity, and death are not sent us by Our Father's hand, are not the orderings of His will, but are the outcome of natural laws operating upon a sinful and distorted humanity, have we not surrendered to the cold and pitiless machinery of laws that most precious thought, that our lives and the lives of our dear ones are in the hand of God; that God's will is constantly exercised in our behalf; that the interests which are dear to us are dear also to Him, and may be brought in faith to Him; have we not, in fact, taken the heart out of prayer, and left only a form of words?" Now, what answer shall I make to this objection? The only answer I can make is this: So far am I from believing that the importance and the reality of prayer are disparaged by our denial that sickness, calamity, and death are God's will for His children, I believe, on the other hand, that no child of God can enter into the joy and preciousness of prayer as fully as he might enter until he does deny that the devilish evils of this world are sent upon a groaning Humanity by the God Whose nature and Whose name is Love. Until he makes that denial in the fullness of his faith; until, with his body racked by pain, with his property melting before his eyes, with his loved ones tossing in fevers or maimed by accidents, with the clods of the hillside dropping on coffins that contain his heart's delights, with the cry of a world in pain and poverty and animalism sounding in his ears — until, with these things about him, he can look straight up into God's face and say: "My Father, my Saviour, my Comforter, none of these things are from Thee or of Thee; Thou hatest them as I hate them; they are foreign to Thee; they are alien and antagonistic to Thy Will; they are the fruits of sin, and the malign deeds of the Devil;" until he can say that, I do not see how he *can* pray without strange and sad misgivings lurking in his heart concerning the very God to Whom he makes his prayer. It would seem to me that he who realizes intelligently the horrors of human calamity and the dreariness of death, who understands the hideous thing of which he speaks when he says, "the sorrows of mankind," and yet who maintains that these things are God's will — the will of Him Who has died for the world — must encounter an embarrassment in prayer which would be insuperable, were it not for the tendency, common among us, to repeat traditional language, without forcing ourselves to inquire into its meaning.

The embarrassment of praying to a God Who is at one and the same time the fountain of a boundless love, and the willing sender of the piteous miseries, the heart-breaking bereavements, the loathsome maladies of mankind, is a greater embarrassment than many a heathen encounters when he prostrates himself before the monstrous image of cruelty which he calls his god. In his conception of that being there are no complications of love. Wrath, cruelty, and rapacious lust for human victims are the harmonious attributes of Moloch. Moloch's heart, in the estimate of his shuddering devotee, is a well of unadulterated ferocity. And when he prays to Moloch, he pleads for mercy as a man might plead with a murderer whose knife is poised above him. There is at least no embarrassment in prayer under those circumstances. But on the other hand there is embarrassment, and a secret misgiving which has led unnumbered persons to abandon prayer, in the conception of a God Who is love; Who pities His children like a Father; Who is more ready to give His Holy Spirit than parents are to give good gifts unto their children; Who knoweth our frame; Who remembereth that we are dust; Who hath borne our griefs and hath carried our sorrows; Who is the Comforter; Who is the Friend of sinners; Who is the Good Shepherd; Who can have compassion on the ignorant and on them that are out of the way — all this, and at the same time, Who by His will, which we are bound to accept, is pouring down upon the good and the evil, the young and the old, the useful and the useless, the strong man, the beautiful wife and mother, the loving son, the sweet daughter, the enchanting and guileless infant, a ceaseless storm of trouble; so that thousands of homes echo with the screams of suffering, the hospital wards are lined with pallid faces, the scenes of accidents are red like the bloody shambles, and men and women are going about bowed with the misery of their trials and weeping for those who will never come back to them. Three hundred thousand persons sleeping in Greenwood to-day! Try to measure the sorrows issuing from those three hundred thousand deaths — yet what are they among so many, or what, even, is death, among the other sorrows of mankind?

Now this is the real embarrassment to prayer; the true stumbling-block. If all Christians knew how many persons are abandoning prayer, having no heart for it, no belief in it, no comfort from it, no sense of logical consistency in it, they would be inclined, as I have been inclined, to ask the reason why. When this great Book of God speaks to us of prayer on almost every page, why have so many ceased to pray? When prayer is one of the fundamental instincts of humanity, when prayer is as natural as love, why have countless men and women sealed their lips toward God, looking up into His face coldly and without a sign? There must be a reason for the decline of prayer, and there is. And I believe the reason is this: the practical difficulty of reconciling the New Testament conception of God's love with the traditional teaching that our earthly evils, calamities, sicknesses, and bereavements are the operations of God's will. Those who have been well grounded in this ancestral tradition, and who possess the additional advantages of submissive dispositions and religious habits of long standing, pray on, meekly and patiently, repressing as temptations of Satan those misgivings which come from time to time when calamities of unusual ferocity make unusual demands on their traditional belief; but others in this age of clear-cut thinking, who have not been so bred in the tradition that the freedom of their thought is shackled, perceiving the anomaly of maintaining the sweet relations of prayer with One by Whose will incessant tortures and sufferings are desolating the earth, simply discard prayer as being itself but a tradition, but the survival of an age of credulity and superstition.

From such a conclusion regarding prayer, a conclusion which discards prayer as obsolescent and irrational, my mind revolts with horror and dismay. No greater calamity can befall a person in this world than that he shall cease to pray. For when he has ceased to pray he has sealed up the very outlet of his soul; he has stifled the natural means of spiritual expression; he has done to his own being a most cruel and disastrous injustice. He was made with an instinct for prayer. Prayer is a characteristic function of the normal man. When he is complete, he prays. To disown prayer, to discard prayer, is a sin against self. It is a form of self-mutilation. Who can ever forget Lord Tennyson's glorious outburst concerning prayer as a part of manhood's birthright? —

> "What are men better than sheep, or goats
> That nourish a blind life within the brain,
> If, knowing God, they lift not hands of prayer —
> Both for themselves and those who call them friend.
> For so the whole round earth is every way
> Bound by gold chains about the feet of God."

Prayer is a duty. Prayer is a comfort. Prayer is a power. *Prayer is a duty commensurate with life itself.* He Who came in great tenderness to visit us, taking upon His preexistent life the very manhood of man, and Who, comprehending in His manhood all man's need, often "continued all night in prayer," has laid this duty upon us, saying that men "ought always to pray and not to faint." The sphere of that duty is commensurate with life itself: "In *everything* with prayer and supplication, let your requests be made known unto God." The man is to spread out his life, to pour out his heart, to breathe out his thoughts before God. Whatever mysteries may cluster about prayer (and how could such a subject possibly be free from lofty and solemn mystery?), this is clear: that prayer is a duty. And what is this but another way of saying that prayer is a God-given instinct never to be repressed without sin. Prayer is expression. Prayer is fellowship. Prayer is friendship. It is our duty; our duty to ourself as much as our duty to God, to pray. Prayer is the intimacy of a boundless confidence, withholding nothing from the Beloved Friend; *in everything* letting the requests be made known, assured that this outpouring of our hearts is in the fullest sense according to His will. Familiar to all is that noble line of the Latin poet:

"I am a man: I deem nothing alien to me that affects humanity."

I remember to have seen that line applied with magnificent effect to the Incarnate Christ: "I — the Christ Incarnate — am a Man. I deem nothing alien to Me that affects Humanity." Christ's Humanity lifts every human interest within the scope of prayer, and makes it our duty as well as our privilege to tell Him all; and there are human interests which we can tell to no one, can explain to no one, but to

Christ; and we tell Him with perfect confidence that He understands.

Prayer is a comfort. "In everything let your requests be made known unto God. And the peace of God, which passeth all understanding, shall guard your hearts and your thoughts in Christ Jesus." "Casting all your care upon Him, for He careth for you." "Is any among you afflicted? Let him pray." It is most certainly true that many of those who have believed that all sickness, calamity, and death are the will of God, sent to punish or sent to educate, have found great comfort in prayer, have learned to kiss what they believed to be the hand that struck them, and to rejoice in the will that bruised and wasted the body; it is true that many have shown both stoicism and submission in prayer to Him by Whom, as they believed, every earthly prospect had been blighted; but it is also true, most terribly true, that unnumbered multitudes, unable to attain this stoicism, have ceased to pray since the iron of sorrow entered into their souls. They look at God in silence; they do not blaspheme, but neither do they pray.

But when a man can deny — in the fullness of faith — that these earthly evils are the will of God, when he can believe that calamity, sickness, and death are as evil to God as they are to us, then the comfort of prayer becomes indeed a peace which passeth all understanding. For then he goes to God without misgivings; he pours out to his Father the pent-up emotions of the heart without the sinister after-thought that he has been confiding in his tormentor; then the great instinct of prayer asserts its natural spontaneity, and nothing can keep him from praying. And the more wildly blows the tempest of life's confusion, the more intensely he clings to God, knowing that in Him is refuge and from Him is strength.

And prayer is a power. "More things are wrought by prayer than this world dreams of." It is a power subjective and objective. It is a subjective power : a power sent *in* to strengthen the spirit of him who prays.

> "We kneel, and all around us seems to lower;
> We rise, and all the distant and the near
> Stands forth in sunny outline, brave and clear.
> We kneel, how weak — we rise, how full of power."

What an inrush of this subjective power comes to him who prays, believing that God is wholly on his side, as against the pain and weariness and sad mischance of life. To such, prayer is often like a vision of God's face.

Glory and light pour, as through some rich window, upon the sombre coloring of life. Courage and hope are quaffed, as with eager lips, from a chalice of crystal. Christ seems to share His Omnipotence with us, for we dare to say: "I can do all things through Christ Which strengtheneth me."

But the power of prayer is objective as well as subjective; effective to accomplish, as well as powerful to sustain. What scope for prayer in every situation! Is our dear one setting out upon a journey? With what wealth of reasonableness may we commit that life to the God Who is the enemy of all evil, lawlessness, calamity and death! Is our dear one stricken with illness? With what reasonableness can we pray that He to Whom all hearts and minds lie open may so calm the mental life of the sufferer, and may so guide the judgment and inspire the skill of those who minister to sickness, that blessed relief and recovery may ensue! Is our dear one or ourself caught in the cyclone of disaster? To whom first shall we go but unto Him, the wonderful Counsellor, the Friend of friends, the Shadow of the rock in the land of weariness? Ah! brothers, for many of us the night is dark, and we are far from home. The moor, the fen, the crag, the torrent, are grievously near and

THE DUTY OF PRAYER. 93

real. Is any among you afflicted? Let him pray! Yes! men ought always to pray and not to faint. Prayer should be a life, and life should be a prayer. When all is over, we shall rejoice if neither pleasure seduced us nor pain shocked us out of prayer.

Can I close these words about prayer more worthily than in the language[1] of one who now is with His Saviour in Paradise — Canon Liddon — perhaps the greatest of all the Canons of St. Paul's: —

"Life is like the summer's day; and in the first fresh morning we do not realize the noonday heat, and at noon we do not think of the shadows lengthening across the plain, and of the setting sun, and of the advancing night. Yet, to each and all, the sunset comes at last, and those who have made most of the day are not unlikely to reflect most bitterly how little they have made of it. Whatever else they may look back upon with thankfulness or with sorrow, it is certain that they will regret no omissions of duty more keenly than neglect of prayer; that they will prize no hours more than those which have been passed, whether in private or in public, before that Throne of Justice and of Grace upon which they hope to gaze throughout eternity."

[1] *Some Elements of Religion*, p. 203.

www.ingramcontent.com/pod-product-compliance
Lightning Source LLC
Chambersburg PA
CBHW020901160426
43192CB00007B/1028